# The Tree of Inspiration

Thoughts to Inspire Your Days

Rajeev Priyadarshi

# About the Tree of Inspiration

The tree of inspiration has many branches, and the words of wisdom in this book are like the leaves on the branches of this tree. These leaves should leave you feeling motivated, enlightened, and – yes – inspired. The branches of the tree of inspiration represent:

3

# The Tree of Inspiration

Like any tree, there are more leaves on some branches than others, but while the tree may not be perfectly balanced... it should help you reach a point of perfect balance in your life.

This book has its origins in my Facebook page, to which I posted my inspirational ideas on an almost daily basis between 2010 and 2015.

*Rajeev*

# Inspirational People

## What we can learn from Famous People

In these celebrity-obsessed times, many of us are influenced by the actions of the rich and famous. But there is another set of famous people who are inspirational in spirit, who are remembered and regarded for their words and deeds regardless of any worldly wealth they may have. Here are just a few of those people...

---

Viktor Frankl was a holocaust survivor who was able to find humor and comfort while going through toughest experience humans have ever suffered! How was he able to do that and what can we learn from him? He was able to do that by having an overarching life-purpose and by using his toughest experience as lessons to achieve his life's purpose. Our sufferings can have a uniquely powerful and empowering meaning for us and we are called to create this unique meaning! If he could do that, we can do that too and that can result in an optimistic and empowering attitude transcending tough experiences and creating a deeply powerful life!

\*\*\*

Mahatma Gandhi's life was his message. Simple living, universal love, integrity, non-violence, self-sacrifice and fearlessness were personified in the life of this great man. If the world could start thinking in the Gandhian way, there would be no wars and unrest. Can we adopt at least one quality from him and become better human beings in the process? Yes, we can!

\*\*\*

# The Tree of Inspiration

In today's world, it is an accepted norm to be crazy-busy. We believe that being busy is the surest way to professional success. But is that really true? Ralph Waldo Emerson once suggested that everyone should simplify their lives. In today's life, letting go of what is unnecessary can help us to focus on the things that matter and can lead us to a more fulfilled – instead of frantic – lives!

***

Let not the joys and sorrows of the moment deter you from pursuing your life-purpose with a single-minded focus. It is important to rejoice in times of joy, and grieve in sadness, but we need to remember that these are temporary. Even life is temporary, but life-purpose endures. Mother Teresa is no more, but her mission continues. Leonardo da Vinci is no more, but Mona Lisa is still here! It is easy to "chill", but is deeply satisfying to define and pursue our life-purpose!

***

Barack Obama once said about the USA, "We might have all come here on different boats, but now we are on the same ship and hence we need to work together to grow and prosper." I'd extend this analogy to our planet. We all came here on different boats of physical, emotional, economic and religious backgrounds, and we did not have any say in this. Why can't we try to co-exist with mutual respect for people who look and think different from us? There cannot be proud of the world we pass on to our children until we learn to co-exist and think of ourselves as a collective whole.

***

The euphoria of success can make us complacent. There is a danger of abandoning the disciplined habits that made us successful. When our happiness is rooted in our daily actions, we can be stable, poised and composed internally...

and still achieve continuous success externally. The great Indian movie icon Amitabh Bachchan has achieved the pinnacle of what any human can achieve in his craft, but he still has the discipline to write his daily blog no matter how tired he is or where he is! He is still very disciplined in his food habits and exercise. This is something to emulate!

\*\*\*

The legendary retailer J C Penney once said that the biggest lesson that he learned was the act of letting go. When we realize that we cannot control all aspects of our lives, either we can frantically try to control the outcome or we can serenely accept what happens to us and focus on our actions and behaviors—irrespective of the outcome. One leads to temporary satisfaction of desires, and the other leads to greater control over oneself.

\*\*\*

Your happiness is your responsibility—not the government's, your spouse's, or your friend's responsibility. When we abdicate this responsibility, we let go of the best gift given to us. Taking ownership of this responsibility is what differentiated Nelson Mandela from everyone else!

\*\*\*

Don't let negative news disturb your inner peace. The selfishness and violence in mankind is not new; it has always been there. But this did not prevent Gandhi, Jesus and Buddha from bringing light to the darkness. We also have an opportunity to make a difference in the lives of people around us by being a stronger force of love and kindness. Keep on sharing, and more will be given to you. Forget about yourself, and be the source of unconditional love for others. Only then you can experience true joy.

## The Tree of Inspiration

It is an irony that we fight for our lives, loved ones, and property, but leave it all behind at the end. No one knows the mystery after death, but that is when we will find out if it was all worth fighting for. Why not focus on love, peace and kindness, irrespective of what is happening around us now? Our inner freedom has nothing to do with our external circumstances. It is widely known that Mandela found more inner freedom in prison than his captors. If he could, why can't we?

# Divine Inspiration

## What we can learn from Religion, Spirituality, God or Mother Nature

You may believe in the divinity of a particular deity, or you may not. But most if not all of us have some form of spirituality, even if we are only in awe of Mother Nature. There is something divine that defines our human nature, so I present my thoughts based on my own divine inspiration...

---

It is difficult to accept that all the happiness we seek from the world is already within us. This difficult realization is a part of the divine plan; this ignorance is what makes the world run and civilization flourish. If we knew that we already have the happiness we seek, then why would we work hard? How can we use this knowledge in our daily life? When things get hectic, relax, knowing that you and your sufferings are a part of His plan. You cannot control every outcome, He controls it. If we can connect to the peace and happiness that comes from divine love, no battle can injure our soul and we become more powerful than our circumstances.

\*\*\*

Set big goals. Have higher standards of personal behavior than the accepted norm. Though this is a scary thought, we need to remember that we are never alone. Our creator is limitless and is always with us. All growth happens with deep faith, lofty dreams and systematically planned hard work.

\*\*\*

Trusting God's will and His plan can solve many of our worry problems!

# The Tree of Inspiration

Divinity is all around us; what we lack is the vision to see it. Every time when you witness the beauty in the world, take a moment to thank the Creator.

***

Faith is the pillar that can give us strength when life seems shaky and uncertain. Just because our logic cannot comprehend the existence of God, this doesn't mean God does not exist. There are frontiers of existence far beyond the boundaries of our knowledge. No matter how trying your challenge, keep walking forward in faith. Feel the joy and bliss that comes from deep faith.

***

The true meaning of life can only come from utilizing our God-given talents to serve the world and make our unique contributions.

***

Some life-battles can't be won just by human will and efforts; they need divine intervention. Prayer and faith are very powerful forces. Having an unshakeable faith in God, powerful self-confidence, and a hard work ethic will make you unstoppable.

***

Respect your parents because they represent God in real life. They might not be perfect, but they love you unconditionally, and I have never seen anyone truly happy who does not respect his or her parents. If you have some anger because of troubled past, let it go, because love conquers anger. Remember that you have limited time on this planet with them, and you will be left only with

10

memories. So Let those memories be about good times well lived... and not about the regrets of unspoken love.

***

There is a bigger purpose for every event in our lives. Sometimes we don't understand it when it happens, but it becomes clear when the time comes. When we trust the divine plan, we don't have to feel sad for the "misfortunes" of life! We get the courage to accept with equanimity anything that life throws at us.

***

Material success and inner happiness are two different things; it is very common to get one without the other. Material success is a measurement of our material contribution to the world. Since God gave us hunger and desire, he expects us to work hard and succeed in the world. But inner happiness is the ultimate goal of the soul, and it is possible to achieve it irrespective of outer circumstances. The magic lies in knowing how to achieve material success and inner happiness.

***

There are some relationships which nourish your soul! These relationships cannot be created by your will and behavior. These relationships are gifts from God, to make your life on this planet worthwhile. As our days get busier, let us not forget to nurture and cultivate these relationships. After all, what is the use of winning that trophy if there is no one to celebrate with you?

***

# The Tree of Inspiration

Fulfilling our life's purpose is our creator's directive to us. This is why we have been given a specific set of emotions and talents. The path is not supposed to be easy and comfortable. But we have also been given free will to either pursue our life's mission or ignore it in favor of comfortable and pleasurable living. Choose wisely!

***

God's love for us and His magnificence is visible in the beauty of His creation! When you know that you have a Father who loves you unconditionally and always protects you, why should you worry? Just let go and let God's plan be manifested through you. Then find the peace within.

***

Humanity has always tested the resolve of people with deep belief. But, it is only divinity that can ask for forgiveness for the very same people who are hurting and crucifying him. If we could love each other like Christ, we'd be the owners of a deep inner bliss much more satisfying than all the wealth of the world. Mutual respect across all differences has always been the need of the hour, but we have been trying to learn it since the dawn of civilization.

***

Of all the things that have brought me ultimate joy, the most important has been my relationship with God. Loving and trusting God's plan can enable us to open our hearts and love everything and everyone around us!

***

# Divine Inspiration

You are a unique child of God, with unique talents and born to shine! Let no one convince you otherwise. You have to believe in your potential to create an impact. People who have given up on their dreams might try to "explain" why it is not possible for you to make a difference. Just listen to the hum of the music in you, and the potential within you, then with deep faith resolve to do whatever it takes to develop and share your gifts so that the world can benefit because you lived here.

***

The creator of the world wanted to store all the love in a safe place so that we could always see love in action; and that safe place was a mother's heart!

***

When you live in accordance with your deepest core values, the opinions of the world will not bother you! Act for the approval of your higher self or God, and not for the whims and fancies of a constantly changing world. The path with values may be very difficult, but walking steadfastly on it will give you an inner peace that no worldly being or thing can ever give you!

***

Sometimes life throws a problem at you that is deeply painful and "unsolvable". Some good strategies to respond: acceptance of the problem, deep love for God, belief in one's ability to stay strong through the problem, and an understanding that the problem is the instrument to transform you and fulfill your life's purpose! Every life-challenge is a stepping stone to helping you find and accomplish your life's mission.

***

# The Tree of Inspiration

When we rely solely on our efforts and talents, there will be times when we find ourselves at our wit's end. Nothing we are doing seems to make any difference. These are the times to pray for God's infinite power to help you in your endeavors. With man this might be impossible, but with God all things are possible.

***

If we compare ourselves to a tree, our beliefs and motives are the roots, and our behaviors, actions and interactions are the branches! When our beliefs are governed by a changeless God and our motive is to live a congruent and authentic life, the roots are deep and strong... and the branches become vibrant, expansive and nourishing for everyone around us. But if our sense of security comes from money, possessions or reputation, we will constantly be worried about losing it all. For permanent happiness, find your security in God and perform your duties as a service to God. Then you can enjoy all your rewards as gifts from God, without the fear of losing them.

***

What can we do when we witness sad and scary happenings throughout the world? We can be a source of strength and comfort for others. Where do we get our strength from? We get our strength from God. We accept that we can never understand the big picture, but we trust our creator who sustains us.

***

I read somewhere that prayer is your message to God, and intuition is God's message to you. Pay attention to your intuition, because sometimes our finite brains cannot comprehend what our intuition always knows.

# Divine Inspiration

Life's situations can never remain the same. There will be crests and troughs, joys and sorrows, incredible company and loneliness! To find true happiness, we need to look inwards and not outwards. The Bible says that the kingdom of God is within you. Gita says that once you know the Self, you don't need anything else to be happy.

***

We are the pen through which God is writing the story of his miracles. We have free will, and hence our personal parable could either be a positive or a negative lesson to demonstrate his presence. By working sincerely on our responsibilities every day with a spirit of calmness and unconditional love, we fulfill our life's mission and exemplify His qualities.

***

Expectations of others will sooner or later lead to disappointment. When we think that someone else is responsible for our happiness, we are bound to be unhappy. We are responsible for our own happiness. Accept with gratitude any kindness, but don't expect it. Trust God but don't expect that His response will always be what you want. He will give us what we need, whether we like it or not, and whether we understand it or not.

***

It is easy to be grateful for the good times, but it is important to be grateful for the tough times too. If we look back at our lives, we might find that the tough times made us who we are. These are the crucibles of life—where we build our character, where we dig deep and find reserves of strength that we did not know we had within us. Next time you have a tough time, don't ask "Why me?" Stare it back squarely in the eye, fight and win. With God and willpower on your side, there is no battle that you cannot win. Sometimes, even if the whole world thinks you have lost a battle, know that you still won, because you became a different person in the process.

***

It is our divine responsibility to protect and work towards our dreams. Dreams are like children, given to us by God. If we don't nurture them, feed them and work on them, they can't grow and become contributing members of society. Every invention that we enjoy and take for granted was once someone's dream; someone who had the courage, strength and persistence to bring it to life. Don't stop dreaming and never give up on your dreams.

***

The true purpose of life is God-realization. Yes, we have to work hard to fulfill our responsibilities in this world. But, to think that any material achievement is going to give us permanent happiness is absurd. We have gotten used to the thrill of pursuit. Once we achieve one milestone, we start pursuing the next. This continues till we die. If we want to break from this loop of constant life-long pursuit, we have to change our perspective dramatically.

***

I feel gratitude for the life that has been given to me, with all its ups and downs. I feel grateful for the family and friends who have taught me and shared their valuable moments with me. I feel grateful to God, who has always given great gifts, sometimes in the form of joys that I cherish and sometimes as painful lessons that I needed to learn.

***

# Divine Inspiration

When we realize our oneness with God, we start loving the present moment and are not concerned with the regrets of the past and the worries about the future. This moment is the best that it could be. To find happiness in the present moment, we need to look inwards and not outwards. The kingdom of God is within us.

*** 

Anyone can achieve bliss by meditating on the divine, by mentally letting go of belongings, by accepting the perfection of the present, and by recognizing that we are enough and we are loved unconditionally by our creator.

***

The thought that everything that happens to us is a part of a bigger divine plan can comfort and assure us during the trials and tribulations of life. When we trust in this divine plan, we know that – while we might be ignorant of the big picture right now – we will be able to see it when the right time comes. When we walk in this faith, we become the source of universal and unconditional love for everyone around us.

***

Spiritual affirmation for the morning: I am the spirit that was never born and that will never die, always joyous and fearless going through an iterative dream journey of multiple lives. I started this journey with nothing and will leave with nothing. Let no worry that troubles me in this incarnation cause me to forget my true entity as an everlasting spirit, always joyous and always free.

***

## The Tree of Inspiration

Our free will can either be our biggest asset or the deadliest weapon of self-destruction. When the will is guided by all-aware divine wisdom, it can lead us to being happy, kind and powerful contributors. When the will is guided by the whims and fancies of the monkey mind, it can lead from one entrapment to another, gradually reducing our freedom to choose wisely and finally leading to self-destruction.

***

We came into the world alone and we will leave it alone. We came here with nothing, and we will leave with nothing. We live life, but we can't understand it. We are ignorant, but we judge others. Respect the mystique of life, and focus on your being rather than your doing. Enjoy the bliss of the present and everything in it, while understanding that it is transitory. Focus on the changeless Truth that can only be comprehended by faith, not logic: where we came from and where we ultimately go back to.

***

Either our lives are completely random or they are part of a divine plan. I don't know the truth. But, I do know that if I believe in the latter, I feel a sense of deep peace, unconditional love, and certainty. Life as short as it is, so why would we not choose inner peace over self-created prison of unlimited desires?

***

Everything in the material world is transitory. Getting attached to what is impermanent is the root cause of sorrow. Desire is a hungry beast which can never be satisfied. Desire and ego are two forces which, when properly channeled, can make the world a better place. But when out of control, they can

# Divine Inspiration

cause some real damage in the world. True happiness can only come from within, from faith, and love with the divine!

\*\*\*

It doesn't take a lot of effort to be a "nobody"—ignoring your God-given talents and being completely subservient to your circumstances. It takes courage to lift your head above the crowd and ignore the negative voices inside and outside you. Identify your divine nature, your unique talent to serve the world, and shine on. There never was anyone like you, and there never will be.

\*\*\*

The only way to religious harmony in the world is through religious tolerance and unconditional acceptance of people's rights to choose their own spiritual path.

\*\*\*

The most frustrating moment in life is when you feel that you have zero control over your situation. That hopeless feeling incapacitates and paralyzes you to inaction. But there is one action you can take during the darkest of the situations, and that is to sincerely pray. Also in most situations, instead to trying to solve the big gigantic problem, try to solve a small part of the problem by taking action. Taking action creates momentum, which – when coupled with faith – can solve life's biggest challenges.

\*\*\*

Growth is life. If we are not growing every day, then the resulting easy life is an escape from our journey towards our divine purpose. If our body and mind are both working, this means our maker wants us to use them to serve others and fulfill our divine destiny. It is easy to have a self-centered relaxed life, just as it is safe for a ship to remain in the harbor, but, a ship is meant to sail and a human life is meant to make a difference.

\*\*\*

Don't let the world prevent you from pursuing your divine purpose. It is by pursuing your divine purpose that you give the world your best gift—an empowered, creatively engaged, contributing, happy and inspirational you. If you give life your best shot, you can rest in peace on your deathbed knowing that the world is a better place because you walked on this planet. Remember that greatness is not just for a few lucky souls, it is a possibility for anyone who can dream.

\*\*\*

True happiness can only come from being aware of the inherent paradox in the universe. There cannot be just one way. Our limited minds can try to explain the miracles of the world only through our limited knowledge and theories. We can fight over how we perceive things to be, unaware that we all have a limited perspective. Can we try to enjoy the miracles of universe without trying to understand them?

\*\*\*

For every point there is a counterpoint. Duality is the way of nature!

# Intergenerational Inspiration

### What Parents, Children and other Family Members can learn from Each Other

As a family man, I understand how inspirational it can be to live within a support network of loved ones. Parents can inspire their children to greatness, and reciprocally those children can inspire their parents (and grandparents) to be grateful for the gift of life. Here follow my thoughts on this intergenerational inspiration...

---

The best things in life are free. Mother's love, father's care, and the bonds between true friends are priceless... yet free. The most important aspects of our lives – who our parents are, when we are born, and when we die –are not controlled by us. With so much of our very foundation not being determined by us, how can we be proud of being self-made? The only response to the wonderful gift of life can be humility and gratitude. Yes, we still need to make right choices and work hard, but only after being thankful for the opportunity to make those choices.

\*\*\*

Truly fortunate are those who get the opportunity to show their love, care and respect for their parents. Today you might get accolades for your achievements, and the seduction of success might create the illusion of being a "self-made" success, but one little slip during those infant years and our stories might not have turned out so good. Take the time to demonstrate your love, care and respect for your parents. They might not respect your opinions, they might have their own ways of living their lives, and they might not have been the best role models for you, but it doesn't matter. Get over your childhood hurts, forgive them if they did not know better, and do whatever is needed to serve them. This is the way to be the role model for your own children.

***

I wish I could wipe away the tears of my kids as they learn to navigate their lives. I wish I could take away the pain of my aging parents. But I do know that my unfulfilled wishes are a part of His plan; a plan that I don't understand. I do know that in the midst of barbaric inhumanity there are kind hearts full of love. I do know that I am not called to understand life but to live it. I do know that I cannot lose hope, because so long I have hope I can still make a positive change in my small way.

***

If you have children, you are truly blessed, because in those little bundles you have been given infinite joy and invaluable lessons. Days spent with children should be cherished like precious treasure. There will be times to share life lessons, time to just listen. Your presence is more important than your presents!

***

We all want happiness now! Then why do we make our happiness dependent upon myriad factors, most of which are not real in the present moment? Happiness is a lot about unlearning, going back to the childlike innocence where we trusted, believed, loved unconditionally, and were happy for no reason. Let us not make happiness a distant goal, but an effortless attitude resulting from genuine inner gratitude for our current situation.

***

# Intergenerational Inspiration

Work needs to be done to feed the family, and work needs to be done to feed the soul. The lucky ones find work that feeds both. For everyone else who focuses on doing only one of these works—either the family or the soul starves. To have a balanced life, we need to plan our week so that we can work on nourish the soul as well as feeding the family.

***

Our effectiveness during the week depends on our relaxation during the weekends. During the weekends, be truly present for the important people in your life. Pursue your hobbies, use household chores and errands as opportunities to bond with family, and please try not to check your work email. Planning the weekend is critical. Make time to smell the roses, time to laugh, time for gratitude, and time for reflection and prayer so that you are truly rejuvenated to grow and succeed during the coming week.

***

Sometimes I wish that time had frozen when I was six and when every little hurt melted in the warm hugs from my dad! I could have been spared the lessons of life and the pain of becoming an adult. But, if that had happened, I could have never experienced the bliss of my own fatherhood! Some of us are truly blessed to have the guidance of our fathers and the opportunity to be a father. If there is a weary heart who always missed the presence of an earthly father, remember that we always have the love, care and blessings of our Heavenly Father!

***

The love of family and responsibility of children is one of the important reasons for the world's progress. Tremendous energy can be generated by the desire to help, support, and nurture your loved ones. This reminds me of the movie

# The Tree of Inspiration

"Cinderella Man", where a reporter asks the winning boxer the secret of his drive, and the hero replies, "Milk!" The desire to feed milk to his children drove him to become a fanatically driven winning champion.

***

Don't be unduly attached to the achievements of your children. Encourage them to do their best, share your lessons, support your children in the best possible way, and celebrate their successes. But living our dreams through our children is a prescription for long-term unhappiness, both for the children and for ourselves. This can be done by never letting go of our own dreams, and by pursuing our passion and unique purpose for our entire lifetime.

***

The cycle of life always repeats itself. When we were were toddlers, we could not have survived without the support and protection of our parents. There will come a time when they'd need our presence and support to live and die with dignity. When that time comes, don't let your limitations stand in the way of your most primary duty as a human. Spend as much time as possible, provide as much emotional and physical support as possible, and be there for them. If you are lucky, you will get that chance, and when it happens... don't let that opportunity slip through your fingers.

# Inspiration through Connection

Our interconnectedness extends outside our immediate family, to encompass friends, work colleagues... and even the random people we meet in the street. This extended network can provide additional inspiration through connection, and in particular—the inspiration to help ourselves by helping others...

---

Even when you are in the throngs of deep pain, you have the ability to reduce the suffering of someone else. When you become committed to serving others, and you forget about yourself, you get connected to a fountain of joy that you never knew existed. Find yourself by losing yourself.

\*\*\*

Research has proven that healthy relationships with other humans are critical for happiness and longevity. But it is difficult to have great relationships with others unless we have a great relationship with our values and ourselves.

\*\*\*

Mutually respectful, affectionate and trusted human relationships are the best gifts we can have in life. Cherish the key relationships in your life, because they make life worth living.

\*\*\*

## The Tree of Inspiration

Everyone wants to be heard, feel that they are understood, and know that they are loved unconditionally. In every relationship, if we can just listen with the intent of truly understanding how someone is feeling, we can give them what every heart is silently screaming for. Today, do not be quick to judge. Listen to at least one person in your life with whom you want to improve your relationship, and watch your relationship rise to the next level.

***

Success in the material world comes through confidence, determination and strong desire. The same traits applied to important relationships can translate to being obstinate, stubborn and controlling—a perfect recipe for a relationship disaster. What is the solution? When away from work, detach yourself completely from work and be a vulnerable, tolerant, open, loving, and humble human who does not have all the answers and is able to laugh at himself.

***

We came to this world with nothing and we will leave with nothing. Our bodies will gain in strength, then gradually lose their vigor, and finally die. Every relationship formed will be left behind. Attachment to this temporary station is the cause of all miseries. So let us enjoy our health, wealth and relationships while they last without getting unduly attached to them. When departing, we can be thankful for the victories and the losses during the great game of life we played.

***

Own your self-esteem. Don't let anyone's rejection bring you down. Our fear of being lonely creates neediness, which forces us into relationships that are not perfect matches. Rejection might be painful but is critical, because it frees up the space to welcome truly nourishing relationships into your life.

## Inspiration through Connection

When you get offended by someone's words, you are acknowledging his or her power over you. Stop giving them that power. Just take an impartial look at the facts and their perception. If there is an opportunity to improve, accept and make changes. If not, ignore and move on after thanking them for their concern. Never increase their importance by getting into a verbal duel. Focus all your attention on love and loving relationships, and eliminate toxic relationships from your life.

\*\*\*

Love and respect are critical for any relationship. If there is no love and respect in a relationship, it is better to let that relationship go in order to open the door for new mutually fulfilling relationships. It all starts with a healthy self-respect and an open heart. Life is too short to spend time with people who bring you down.

\*\*\*

When you have great relationships, weekends are more fun, conversations are authentic, and the overall quality of life is phenomenal.

\*\*\*

I feel grateful for the amazing friends in my life. There are friends who inspire me with their thoughts, actions and achievements. There are friends with whom I have shared many wonderful moments of fun and laughter. There are friends who are so centered and peaceful that just talking to them brings me inner joy and calmness. There are friends whom you can call at 3:00 am and they will be there for you, no matter what. Cherish the friends and friendships that make your life a fun-filled, inspiring and fulfilling adventure.

\*\*\*

# The Tree of Inspiration

The richness of life is directly proportional to the richness of our human connections. This is as true today as it was in the pre-historic times.

***

Every day we meet multiple people: in the store, in the traffic, or at the restaurant. Everyone has a story, everyone is fighting his or her own battles, and everyone needs a little love and consideration. If we can take a break from our automatic busy lives, and be interested in their stories, we can realize our own humanity and our human connection to the world around us. Focus more on being interested than being interesting and you will find your truly connected and happy soul.

***

In the hurry to improve our circumstances, we sometimes forget to accept and enjoy what we have. Let us pause to acknowledge the abundance and grace all around us and be truly grateful for it. Reach out to someone who needs a little compassion, care and love today. It is the human connection which makes life worthwhile.

***

Great friends are the best blessings that you can have in life. They truly make the journey enjoyable, they are there during the tough times, and sometimes they tell you what you need to hear when you don't want to listen. I am truly grateful for the wonderful friends I am blessed with.

***

# Inspiration through Connection

What achievement can be bigger than bringing a smile to a sad heart or comforting a grieving soul? We are all connected at a much deeper level than we realize. There is no joy except in connecting, sharing and helping our fellow travelers on this journey called life.

***

The most important determinant of your success in life is your ability to connect with people: being genuinely interested in others, keeping promises, and being a class act. If you want good friends in your life, be a great friend.

***

Everyone you meet today has a story to share, has a challenge to overcome, and has a need to be validated. If you can take a moment away from your story, your challenge, and your need to be validated, you can focus on someone else and listen to their story, understand their challenge, and validate them. You will not only make their day brighter, but you will also come back with renewed appreciation for your own life.

***

Open your eyes of compassion, so that you can feel the emotions of the people you encounter every day. A kind word with sincerity and understanding can brighten someone's day and lighten their load. It can make us feel more alive and make our days more purposeful.

***

# The Tree of Inspiration

Consider yourself incredibly lucky if you can share a laugh, discuss a thought, and break bread with your friends, because this is the only true wealth!

***

Treating everyone that you meet today with emotional and verbal kindness is the best thing you can do for your emotional well-being today. When two cells within our body fight and compete, it is called cancer, and it destroys us. Similarly, when we as humans are antagonistic to each other, we destroy our collective consciousness of humanity. Be kind, be good, and be happy.

***

Every time you go through a tough situation, it can make you very pessimistic and can negatively affect your self-confidence. During these moments remember that you are not alone, that these situations are temporary, and that God has a unique plan for you. Though it might seem easier to be isolated, try to reach out to friends and support groups. You will be pleasantly surprised by the strengths, insight, and self-confidence that you get from connecting with others!

***

Keeping promises is one of the most critical tests of integrity. Habitually breaking promises erodes the trust in any relationship. For long-term relationship success and a stellar reputation, develop the habit of under-promising and over-delivering. If we don't follow through on the promises to ourselves, we gradually lose our self-respect, self-confidence, and self-control.

***

## Inspiration through Connection

Never let the pressures of life dampen the passion in your relationships. If there is one thing that can strengthen every other aspect of life, it is the level of passion in your primary relationship. We prepare a lot for the wedding, but do not prepare enough for the marriage. Focus on the little things in everyday life, which – if ignored – can gradually eat away the foundation of any relationship.

\*\*\*

It is difficult to connect with the world when we are in the midst of our own private battles. But these are precisely the moments when we need to connect. By inspiring others, we find the strength to persist and we achieve our own internal and external victories.

\*\*\*

Life is short. Do what you love, and if you can't... love what you do. Make a difference in others' lives by helping them, loving them and accepting them as they are. Make sure you stand for something that is positive, inspiring and instrumental in the betterment of the world. This can only be done by understanding our unique abilities and utilizing them to serve the world in a way only we can do.

\*\*\*

We are all here to play our very own specific role, but the details of that role are given to us only in the form of hidden clues. If we can identify our strengths and passions, and use them creatively to add value to others, we will find our life-vocation. This can make our life simple, fun and completely rejuvenating. To make this journey complete, you'd also need a support structure populated by people with complementary strengths. Try this and you will be amazed at the sheer happiness you can derive from pursuing your calling.

# The Tree of Inspiration

Sharing is critical for growth. Ensure that a part of what you receive is shared with others who need help. By sharing, you validate your trust in the divine providence, which ensures your achievements. Sharing needs to be done happily, gratefully and discreetly without any hidden agenda or expectation.

***

If you are seeking completeness outside of yourself, you will always be dissatisfied. Thinking that your significant other is going to make you complete is a prescription for unhappiness. You are a complete person, and so is your partner, and you both choose to be in an interdependent relationship to enhance your already-happy lives. Similarly, blaming your partner for your unhappiness is futile, since it is your responsibility to find and practice happiness.

***

We are all here for too short a time to hold grudges. If someone has belittled you, use that hurt and anger to improve yourself to reach the next level, but forgive the person. When you hold a grudge, you are punishing yourself for someone else's mistakes.

***

When you stop pushing for what you want, and start asking how you may serve, you open yourself to infinite possibilities. We are much more capable and powerful than our limited desires. Be flexible, be open, be of service, be generous, and watch the law of reciprocity fill you up with abundance.

***

## Inspiration through Connection

Speak faith and confidence into someone's heart today. Be that ray of hope in the life of someone today. Be that friend who can lift someone today. There are days we need to be lifted and there are days we are called to lift! Let today be the day you make a difference in someone's life.

# Inner Inspiration

What we can learn from our Internal Intuition and our Hearts

Sharing with, and caring for other people is all very well, but we also shouldn't lose our sense of self. Who am I? What do I believe in? Being mindful of oneself and listening to one's own inner voice does not necessarily have to mean being selfish, as I now explain...

---

Listen to your heart. Your heart always knows the right path. We can complicate our decision processes through complex calculations of the brain yet never be sure of our decisions. By trusting your heart and intuition, you are following your own internal GPS that always takes you to your correct destination.

*** 

We humans have been given the gift of free will. When we ignore our core values and try to be in sync with the latest and coolest fads, we are abdicating our gift and trying to live someone else's life. Find your voice, identify your values, and live your own life proudly and authentically. There is not going to be another "you", and hence there is no point in living your one life in accordance to the diktats of the multitude.

***

As I look back over the years gone by, I wonder about the many times I was wrong in my decisions. When facing difficult decisions, don't be afraid to ask for advice from experts and others who have been successful in the same pursuit. It can save you a ton in time and money. I was lucky to have some great advice at the right time to turn things around, and now I offer my advice—always follow your heart and do the right thing.

***

Take some time to tell the important people in your life about how important they are. Life is very short, and you might not get a chance to say in words what your heart always knows. Let us not be in a hurry to reach somewhere so fast that we forget the precious fleeting moments that pass us by. Live in the now, my friends, because this is the only moment that you will ever have.

***

Don't jump into battles to prove who is right in your daily conversations. Everyone is right in their own way, and I am yet to find a person who thinks he is wrong. If you strongly believe in your heart about the rightness of your cause, do speak your voice and take action. Some will agree, some will not, and some don't care. While in some situations we do need to discuss to come to a consensus, in many cases it is an exercise in futility. If your actions can provide positive proof, why waste your time trying to convince others?

***

Find your own voice, choose your own destination, and understand your own self. We are all here in this drama to play our own roles. It is important to identify your own goals and the life-purposes that your heart always knows (but your brain often refuses to listen). Only in hindsight can we learn the most effective path from others who are successful in a particular pursuit.

***

# Inner Inspiration

Don't let the noise of the world drown your voice. It is self-evident that all of us need to be heard, but it is really tragic when we cannot hear our own voices. The voiceless mutterings within our hearts, the silence of suppressed dreams, and the gentle tug within our soul—they all need to be heard by us. When we pay attention to these messages and act on them, we give ourselves and the world a great gift: the gift of a happy and limitless being.

***

It is a challenge to be calmly active or actively calm; to have the right balance of ambition and contentment; to know that all you need to be happy is within you. The heart knows the truth, but the ambitious mind wants to reach one more milestone, climb one more hill, as if achievement is critical to happiness.

***

In the loud din of life, do not lose touch with the silent music constantly playing within your heart. It is that music that truly defines you and makes you a unique incredible gift to the world.

***

Never underestimate the power of will! When you trust your heart and walk with certainty and belief, you can transcend all obstacles. Surround yourself with people, books and symbols which inspire you! Act as if you can never fail! Be the inspiration that the world needs!

***

## The Tree of Inspiration

We all come to a point in life where we realize that we have to be independent of people's opinions about us. The world's opinion is very fickle; there will be times we get bouquets and times when we get brickbats, and at the end... none of these matter. The only way to happiness is to walk confidently in the direction your heart leads you.

***

Don't be afraid of walking on a solitary path with your dream as your sole companion. There will surely be periods of self-doubt and questions about your sanity, but you have to keep on moving forward. Life is too short to walk on someone else's path.

***

Each one of us is here to play a unique role in this life. We have been given some unique talents, a unique perspective on the world, and a unique set of emotions. If we can pause and contemplate inwards, we can find our true calling—our life purpose or Dharma. This is our unique song in the orchestra of life. This is our unique contribution to the world. This is the source of unique unfathomable joy in our lives.

***

Life can be confusing with its twists and turns and the deluge of constantly conflicting information. Amidst the chaos, we need to connect to the quiet place within us—the seat of peace, contentment and gratitude. The stronger the connection, the more stable we can be in this unstable world.

***

# Inner Inspiration

No matter how much you achieve on the outside, you can truly be happy only if you achieve on the inside. A big achievement on the inside is to realize the greatness, happiness and peace with which you were born.

***

There are infinite ways of living life. Find a way that is uniquely suited to your values, temperament and goals... then walk on your path fearlessly. Find and be your authentic self, because everyone else is already taken.

***

I remember being teased and being called names in school. Though not their intention, I now realize that they did me a huge favor. I learned very early to be independent of people's opinions about me. It gave me immense freedom to pursue what I want and not what everybody else wants from me. You cannot be free if you are attached to the label of being the nicest guy or gal around.

***

Be willing to defy the conventions to act in accordance with your convictions. Be willing to travel the uncharted path. Be willing to listen and dance to the music inside you, irrespective of the noise outside. This is your solitary journey, where co-passengers may come and go, but the destination cannot and should not change.

***

# The Tree of Inspiration

Within each one of us there is a place of tranquility and deep placidity. So long we are connected to this place, there can be no battles that we can't win, no calamities that we can't conquer calmly.

***

Loving yourself is not egoistic, narcissistic or cocky. It conveys respect for the wisdom that created you. Unless you love yourself unconditionally, you cannot truly love anyone else or fulfill the mission that you were born for.

***

Find your unique rhythm in life. It is important to know ourselves, our strengths, our weaknesses, our passions and our values. Using our own uniqueness, we can create our own ways of living, which can truly make us happy. Too often we try to live others' lives, and in the process we get frustrated. Now is the time to sing our own song, dance to our tune, and forget about people watching and judging.

***

Do not give up on your dreams, even if everything seems stacked against you. Strengthen your resolve and fuel your desire to break through all obstacles. The biggest enemy is not outside, but within us. It tells us that we are nothing, and questions our abilities. Believe in yourself and your abilities, and persist in your pursuit with a single-minded focus. You will win, and nothing can stop you.

***

The meaning of your life has to be created by you. It is not going to magically fall in your lap. By taking responsibility for your life and its meaning, you become the

# Inner Inspiration

creator of your own happiness, irrespective of your external circumstances! Take control of this power to create your own destiny.

***

No one is responsible for your happiness and success except you. We can complain all day about our environment, our government and our misfortunes, but there are people who have transcended all limitations to create a happy, successful and purposeful life. If they can, why can't we?

***

When you go deep into the inner realms of your core, and you are able to identify your life's purpose and commit to it, the entire universe conspires to make you successful. Just be focused on the ultimate goal, ignore the chatter all around, don't be drawn to a specific path, be open to infinite possibilities, and then surely and certainly you will attain your goal.

***

To be successful in the material world, one needs to be deeply connected to the outer environment. But to be truly happy and peaceful, one needs to be deeply connected to one's inner world. The key is to find the right balance between external engagements and inner solitude.

***

Be clear about who you are, what you stand for, where you are going and why that destination is important for you. Multiplicity of simultaneous destinations is a sure prescription for confusion and inaction. Clarity of purpose, articulation of

# The Tree of Inspiration

your belief and willingness to surrender to your passion has and will move mountains!

***

You are the painter of your own masterpiece on the canvas of your life. You have been given the required skills, the tools and the canvas, but you have to exercise your will to create your own unique legacy. Don't let the trivialities of life distract you from your mission.

***

Beware of the negative self-communication in your head regarding situations and people. By having positive thoughts about people, we can draw out the positive qualities from almost everyone. Similarly, by having positive thoughts about situations, we are able to use our creativity to transform any situation towards a positive outcome.

***

Our emotions can be our best friends or our worst enemies. If you feel strongly about something, think of ways you can channel that emotion to go to the next level or to create something unique. The history of the world is the history of emotional people who leveraged their emotions to make a difference.

# Inspiration from Meditation

## What we can learn by Sitting Still and Contemplating

One very effective way of getting in touch with one's own inner self is through a dedication to meditation; simply sitting still and listening to our own hearts. Here's how you can gain inspiration from meditation...

---

Meditation is the secret sauce for a truly happy life.

***

One habit which helps me to achieve balance is to have some time (2-3 hours every week) to just let go of my to-do lists, to let go of my expectations, and to stop trying to control outcomes. This time is to take a walk in the nature, to laugh with kids or just to meditate in gratitude. This is the time to accept and appreciate life, no matter how it is. This is the time to be a source of love, kindness and abundance for everyone around you. This is the time to breathe and soak in the present moment, reflecting on the transience of life and possessions.

***

It is true that we don't need much to be happy. Happiness comes when we connect deeply inwards with our internal universal consciousness through meditation. However, it is also true that the human mind – unless driven towards a unique life-purpose – atrophies in laziness and pettiness. The key is to find the right balance, to move towards your own goal on your own path, all the while enjoying the bliss of present moment and the journey.

# The Tree of Inspiration

Every day has its own challenges and moments of joy, but true happiness can be experienced at any moment—despite any external adversity. Through the practice of daily meditation, you can connect to the inner oasis of peace within you... totally insulated from the tsunamis of life. As the day progresses, and you get busy, try to remain connected with that peace while performing your actions. Learning this simple habit could be the best gift you ever receive!

***

When one feels truly happy after a good meditation practice, he wants to put in his best efforts on his work—not because of the rewards it brings, but because he gets a strong desire to serve others. When we have passion for our work, the whole world benefits immensely. Work becomes an end in itself, not a means to an end. I agree with Wayne Dyer when he says, there is no way to happiness, happiness is the way!

***

Don't let anyone or any situation steal your confidence, belief and hope. Performing a simple act that you are good at, contributing to others' lives, discussing with a mentor, meditation, prayer and just rest and relaxation are some of the strategies to rejuvenate us during tough times. Remember that tough times never last... but tough people do.

***

Our hearts crave for unconditional love and connection. But human love is generally conditional and dependent upon a variety of factors. By having a daily meditation practice, one can uncover the key to divine bliss—which is unconditional and depends only on one's effort and grace. It is like a switch that you can turn on to get connected to infinite peace and bliss. Imagine the freedom when your happiness becomes independent of external factors.

\*\*\*

Start the day with gratitude, optimism, determination, and a plan. Face the day like a self-confident yet compassionate warrior. The evening meal is a time of bonding, sharing stories and creating memories. End the day again with gratitude for life, its comforts, relationships, and for a fruitful day. Don't go to bed without connecting to your inner peace through a silent prayer or meditation!

\*\*\*

Being busy doesn't always equate to progress. Sometimes, progress can be made by being still. By being still, we can listen to our inner calling and choose actions that can lead us towards our specific life-purpose.

\*\*\*

The secret of inner happiness lies in the tranquil mind. When we focus on our being and not our doing, we can be aware of the miracles all around us. When we realize that the world was a beautiful place before we came here, and it will remain a beautiful place after we leave, we feel humbled by the magnificence of the creation. Being grateful for being here and participating in the process can be a source of real inner joy.

\*\*\*

Nothing in life has any meaning other than the meaning we assign to it. If that is the case, why can't we assign empowering meanings to everything that we have in our life? In the worst case, it makes us feel better. In the best case, it helps us to transcend our limitations to create a phenomenal transformation within and around us.

***

We can't achieve anything worthwhile if our minds are drowning in a torrent of trivial trifles. To achieve anything that we can be proud of, we need to simplify our lives and focus all our attention on the few things that matter. Most of the time, it is not the lack of talent which is the problem, it is the lack of determination and attention.

# Inspirational Habits

Meditation is a good habit to have, but there are other ritualistic behaviors that we can perform habitually each and every day in order to become more inspired. Here are some of the benefits of daily discipline...

---

Happiness is not to be pursued, but created and realized from within. By having daily happiness rituals, we can create a happy life. The habit of gratitude, looking for the positive in any situation, performing daily random acts of kindness, meditation, physical exercise, and a sense of personal values and direction are some habits which − if practiced daily − would lead to overall increase in happiness levels and improve the quality of our lives.

***

All great achievements are the result of daily discipline. Your daily habits might seem inconsequential, but over a period of time can lead to massive changes. We just need faith, confidence and a vision of a meaningful goal to inspire and energize us to pursue our daily discipline. Disciplined company helps, but the bulk of the load needs to be carried by ourselves.

***

As we pursue our goals, the journey can be solitary, tough and stressful. We need to adopt daily relaxation habits to rejuvenate us. What is your favorite way to relax?

# The Tree of Inspiration

Whenever you have a choice, getting into the habit of choosing an option which requires courage can be a wonderful way to develop your self-confidence.

***

Happiness is in appreciation of the simple gifts of life. Simplifying your life to a few ground rules and habits can exponentially increase your happiness. Sometimes it is as simple as saying "Don't worry, be happy!"

***

Discomfort is the friend of growth. If we can get into a daily habit of performing just one action which scares us or makes us uncomfortable, we will be on the sure and steady path of growth.

***

Confidence is the most critical asset required for any achievement. There are some people, habits and environment that increase our confidence. It is important that every day we a) meet at least one person who builds our confidence, b) develop at least one habit which strengthens our confidence, and c) make at least one change in our environment which bolsters our confidence. Growth is an iterative process, and these daily disciplined actions result in massive success over a period of time.

***

Happiness research has shown that a lifetime habit of goal-setting is important for happiness. Happiness doesn't just come from goals, but from the journey to their fulfillment. The goals have to be meaningful for you, and in-line with your core-values.

***

Our daily habits are the most accurate predictor of our future. Are your habits carefully chosen to give you a life of great health, strong relationships, phenomenal success, and deep inner happiness? If not, choose your habits carefully and stick to them. Your habits constitute the rungs of the ladder to your powerful future.

***

Focus on your daily habits. Are they helping you to be a better person and a better contributor? Are they helping you to have better health? Are they helping you to have better relationships? Are they helping you to feel fulfilled and self-controlled? If yes, continue with them. If not, replace them with better habits. Our long term destiny is controlled by the daily habits that can make us or break us!

***

Gratitude is the most important habit for happiness. Every person in the world, no matter how pathetic his or her situation is, has reasons to be grateful. When we focus on what we have, we create the attitude of abundance and expansion that helps us to grow further. Having a daily gratitude ritual, where we can reflect on the ten things we are grateful for, can do wonders to increase our happiness levels.

***

# The Tree of Inspiration

The human mind and body need to be constantly stretched. Being very comfortable and complacent ultimately leads to decay and disintegration of humans and organizations. Every day is an opportunity to learn something new, try something new, and share something new.

***

Uncertainty about the future leads to anxiety, and certainty about the future leads to boredom. The key to a balanced, happy, and exciting life is to acknowledge and pursue uncertainty on a foundation of self-controlled certainty. For example, you can use the certainty of your deep spiritual faith and self-controlled daily routines to pursue the excitement of ambition but uncertain dreams!

***

There are times to strive and there are times to let go. There are times to work on creating an empowering future, and there are times to enjoy the bliss of the present. There are days when you eat to live, and there are days when you live to eat. Variety is the essence of life.

# A Moment of Inspiration

Inspirational Habits were all about how we can be inspired each and every day, and I have more to say about how we can be inspired in the present moment by working our way through life one step at a time...

---

Today is a gift, let us not spend all of it preparing for tomorrow or remembering about yesterday! Hug your loved ones tighter, feel the bliss of togetherness and the magic of love. Take a moment to be thankful for everything that adds value to our lives which we take for granted.

***

There is no happiness bigger than acknowledging the greatness of a single moment. A moment of gratitude, a moment of unconditional love. A moment of divine grace. The beauty of life lies in being completely present in these moments.

***

Finding bliss in the present moment is the best gift you can give yourself.

***

The best way to be prepared for the future is to do, in the very best way, what needs to be done today. Use the passion for your future dreams to get all the tough tasks done as soon as possible. Daily consistent work can lead to miraculous results.

***

Our life today is the result of the choices we made yesterday. If we want tomorrow to be different from today, we need to examine our conscious and unconscious choices and make changes in-line with the future we want to create.

***

Bliss is that momentary feeling when we are totally grounded in the present, when there are no thoughts about yesterdays or tomorrows, when we are completely content with our current state. We all have those moments scattered throughout the journey of life, but we are not completely aware of them. The goal is to increase our awareness of these moments... and be grateful for them.

***

People who wait for the perfect time to start don't accomplish much. There will never be a perfect time for any start. We have to start with our uncertainties and our challenges, constantly monitor our progress, and make course corrections as necessary. Yes, there is something called the right time for the right action, but too often we over analyze and second-guess ourselves as the right time simply slips away. Start sooner, and start often!

***

# A Moment of Inspiration

Every day starts with a promise that can be frittered away by regrets of yesterday and the worries of tomorrow. Today, let us ensure that we love unconditionally, are true to our core values, and work hard to earn our daily bread.

***

Everything that we do takes us either towards our life purpose or away from it. Daily consistent action towards one's purpose can create a miraculous impact over time. Carpe Diem! (Seize the Day)

***

Every morning comes with a new promise of a new achievement, a new learning opportunity, or a new contribution. Take charge of this day, don't be frazzled by the failures of yesterday, and walk boldly in the direction of your dreams. There is no failure except in giving up. Be the force of positive change that you were designed to be. Every impossible task has been achieved through relentless imagination and consistent effort.

***

Every day has a unique value in terms of the progress made, learning receive, and the smiles shared. There are some days when it is a struggle to take one step forward, and then there are some days when you are galloping in your zone. No matter how the day is, if you have done your best to share a smile and make some progress, you can lie in bed with the satisfaction of having fully lived another precious day.

***

# The Tree of Inspiration

It is possible that great moments slip through our fingers without our complete awareness and appreciation of those moments. One way to ensure we don't sleepwalk through life is to spend some time each day, before going to bed, to reflect and journal on the experiences and lessons of the day... and to express our gratitude for those experiences.

***

There will never be a perfect time to start something good, except now. If you feel strongly about anything, take action. The road to hell is paved with good intentions.

***

A lot of people postpone living life until they achieve the next milestone, then the next milestone, and so on. By the time they achieve all their life-goals, they are too tired and old to enjoy anything, and they look back with sadness at the golden moments that are now gone forever. Don't let that be the case with you. Absorb the magic of every moment. Find one or two activities that give you the feeling of complete bliss, and schedule those activities on a weekly basis. These appointments with your happiness need to be non-negotiable. Keep on pursuing your goals and serving others while keeping yourself rejuvenated.

***

Long term happiness does not come from big achievements, it comes from celebrating the little wins every day. When we express gratitude for the small but priceless gifts that many take for granted, we sow the seeds of abundance in our lives, and it is this mindset that creates the feeling of fulfillment and completeness.

# A Moment of Inspiration

When you stop worrying about the things you cannot control, you suddenly get huge energy to focus your actions and behaviors on the things you can control. You can use all your energy and your unique talents to serve others with a spirit of gratitude for the ability to do so. Then the goal shifts from a distant horizon to a feeling of contentment for each day lived well!

*** 

Every day we make choices – sometimes consciously, but most of the time unconsciously – to be happy or indifferent or sad, to accept our role as victor or victim, to be thankful or dissatisfied, to make a difference or to accept the status quo. Today, you can make choices that empower you. Will you?

*** 

In order to create the perfect product, in order to choose the perfect time to take action, and in order to be perfectly happy, we sometimes let go of the countless daily opportunities to improve a little, to take small steps in the right direction, and to celebrate our little moments of happiness. Seize each moment, my friend, because this moment is all that we will ever have.

# Inspired by Dreams

## What we can learn by having Goals and literally "Living the Dream"

While we can learn to live one day at a time and be present in each and every moment, we can find tremendous inspiration in aiming high and trying to reach our ultimate end goals. Here's what happens when you dare to dream...

---

Dream big dreams and believe in your ability to make them happen. The probability of you achieving your dreams is proportional to the intensity of your desire and the depth of your belief. You have to protect and nurture your dream. If you can see it, you can be it.

***

Don't let your doubts and fears control you. Their presence indicates that you are dreaming big dreams. Develop the courage to move forward in spite of your fears. Trust your dreams. If you have been given a dream, then you have also been given the strength to bring it to life. Move forward with courage and do not stop till you achieve your dreams.

***

Dreams drive achievements. While setting your dream goals, ensure that you have a very strong "Why?" for each goal. These "Whys" are going to energize you when the going gets tough. When you make plans to achieve your goals, break up those plans into simple daily routines and disciplines. The simpler the routine, the easier it is to stick to it. Track and tweak your routines on a weekly basis until you achieve your dreams.

# The Tree of Inspiration

Dream no ordinary dreams. Dream dreams much bigger than anyone can imagine. Ordinary dreams require you to work harder and smarter, but when you shoot for an impossible dream you have to become a completely different person. And that, my friends, is way more exciting.

***

The journey of a dreamer is tough. He gets ridiculed, his sanity is questioned, and often his quest is a lonely one. But, his dream fuels him to plod on further and further against all odds. One day, he achieves his dream and he is called an "overnight success". He smiles inside, remembers the journey, and silently says, "If only they knew!"

***

If people are not laughing at your dreams, then you are not dreaming big enough dreams. Own your dreams and commit to your plan. Let no icy winds, storms, earthquakes of life, or ridicules of society distract you from your chosen path. A meaningful and fulfilled life is never easy; it is our very struggle that defines our character and our life's message.

***

The essence of life is in constantly stretching our limits, climbing greater heights, and being happy during the journey. Think about your purpose in life, decide on what actions you need to take this week to be closer to your purpose, and then just take those actions. Consistent and persistent small actions performed regularly can create a gigantic impact. Keep smiling, keep dreaming, and keep working to realize those dreams.

***

# Inspired by Dreams

When you pursue a life of discipline, passion and growth you will make some people uncomfortable. It reminds them of their own unused talents and unfulfilled dreams. But, you cannot let their discomfort dampen your resolve. When you persist against all odds along a road less traveled, to fulfill your life-mission, you bring hope to many more and you inspire them to pursue their dreams. You just have one life, so make it count.

*** 

We often postpone pursuing our calling—citing very practical reasons like I need to save enough money or I will wait until the kids go to college. However, there is a middle path between the extremes of foolhardy risk and the continuous postponement of pursuing your calling. No matter how busy we are, we can always take small steps in the direction of our dreams. It might take some time and adjustment, but arriving late is better than never arriving at all. Avoid perfectionist plans which force you to inaction, and choose small practical steps to slowly and steadily achieve your dreams.

*** 

Your self-doubt can rob you of your destiny. It can steal from the world all your potential contribution. Your self-doubt will appear every time you dream big, but you have to shred your self-doubt to pieces and move forward with certainty. If you have conquered the enemy within, the enemy without can do you no harm. Move forward no matter how many times you fall, because living is in moving forward.

*** 

Everyone says that stress is injurious for health, and that we should not worry too much since the stress might kill us. While I don't disagree with this fact, I have found that if I worry too much about my worries, my stress and my longevity, I choose options which are comfortable and easy. While this might reduce stress, it also reduces the excitement that comes from a life of growth, contribution and fulfillment. Be clear about your dreams, and awaken the giant within you. Don't be afraid of failure or success, but be very afraid of an unlived life, silenced dreams, and the regrets of not believing in yourself. It is not about how many breaths you take, it is about the moments that take your breath away.

***

It is often darkest before dawn. When you are working hard to achieve a worthy goal, often it becomes very tough to believe in the plausibility of your dreams, so giving up on your dreams seems to be the most logical choice. But history has been made, and is being made, by the people who had impossible dreams. Never give up on your dreams, because if you are dreaming... you are living!

***

Willingness to fail and not be afraid of looking stupid is a key ingredient for achieving success. We are afraid of what society will think, and in the process we quash all our dreams. Here is a reality check. There is nothing called society, it is merely a collection of people just like you, worried about the opinions of everyone else. Forget about opinions, and just go for your dreams. You just have one life.

***

As you cross from your comfort zone towards the untrodden path of your dreams, you will have the company of two entities – your doubts and your fears – that will question your dreams and your abilities. But you've got to dig deep, have faith, and keep on moving in the direction of your dreams... no matter what.

# Inspired by Dreams

Have you stopped believing in your dreams because of past failures? Break the spell by committing to small achievable goals. As you start achieving, gradually increase the level of your goals. Never lose your momentum, optimism, confidence and faith, no matter how tough the situation gets.

***

Lucky is the person who has a goal to shoot for. This gives direction to life, enthusiasm in day-to-day living, and a sense of optimistic well-being. A life without a worthwhile goal gets frittered away in useless arguments, unhealthy habits governed solely by sense pleasures, and a general sense of pessimistic apathy. If you want a healthy and fruitful life, always be pursuing a goal that is uniquely meaningful for you; and while you are at it, make sure you enjoy the journey.

***

When we are very focused on a very specific goal and a very specific path to reach it, we often close our minds to the infinite possibilities that might help us to reach our goals faster. Analyzing the hidden needs behind why we seek specific goals can help us focus on those needs. So with those needs in the back of your mind, look at every situation in your life as an opportunity to fulfill them! Sometimes the link is not very clear, and you have to think creatively. This approach may help you to reach your goals faster, without much anxiety, and you might achieve success beyond your wildest dreams.

***

People who pursue perfection are unhappy for most of their lives. Don't worry if your goals are not perfect. Pay attention to what you want, write it down, take action, and tweak your efforts until you achieve your aims. Celebrate your achievement and then set new goals. While pursuing your goals, enjoy the journey, the company, and the moments with love and gratitude. We have one life—let us make it count.

# Inspiring Working and Wealth

## What we can learn from Business, Economics and Work in the Material World

What many of us dream for is worldly wealth, and we work hard to accumulate it. There's nothing wrong with this providing we also follow a more purposeful pursuit—the pursuit of happiness for ourselves and for others. These are my thoughts on how we can be inspired because of (and despite) our economic accomplishments...

---

Any person who has a job that he truly loves, and that can put food on the table, is a very lucky person. Having a job that you love is like going on a daily vacation and getting paid for it. Finding such a job can be a long arduous pursuit and can involve multiple trials, but is totally worth it.

***

Money is like water—you cannot live without it. Water when stagnant becomes unfit for drinking, and money when hoarded and not shared prevents growth. The easiest way to become rich ethically is to focus on value creation for others, and by being prudent with the money you have. Having an abundant, grateful and sharing mindset tends to be a magnet for the creation of wealth.

***

In business, don't be satisfied with "good enough". Be constantly on the lookout for continuous improvement in processes, people, products and services. Pay close attention to what the internal and external clients are saying, and adapt to provide a better level of client satisfaction. There is no such thing as perfection, but there is just continuous daily progress.

# The Tree of Inspiration

Life becomes easier when you stop holding on tight your belongings and your emotions. Share your wealth with others who are less fortunate than you, and let go of the negative emotions that hold you back. As you take these actions, you will experience real freedom and you will witness more abundance flowing in your life. Try grabbing water with a tight fist, and you will remain thirsty. The same is true for inner freedom, wealth and happiness.

***

There are days when you win and there are days when you lose. Win or lose, we need to maintain the rhythm of our work and contributions. There is no inner victory other than a day's work done to the best of our abilities!

***

Let not your success seduce you to complacency. Keep working on your craft, on your unique ability, and on your life purpose until the day you die!

***

Your work is your signature. Your work makes a difference in the lives of others. Your work is a channel for your talents and creativity. Don't take your work for granted; it is a privilege to be able to contribute. No matter what your work is, you have the ability to create a masterpiece and be a positive inspiring example for others.

***

The desire to serve and contribute to the lives of others is the foundation of every successful business or individual.

# Inspiring Working and Wealth

Positional leadership is transactional and not effective in the long run. In the Information Age, the only kind of leadership that is effective is relational leadership. To lead organizations, we need to be visionary. The ability to articulate a future which inspires the team requires us to build a relationship of trust with the team and to be practical and aware of the realities of business, humans and environment. Leadership is not just for the person at the top—people at every level can be, and need to be transformational leaders.

***

Popular culture has glamorized self-gratification and unrestricted pleasure, but in reality this is just one aspect of life. Disciplined work is not merely a way to earn and finance our pleasurable pursuits; disciplined work in your area of expertise and passion is an end in itself. It is the door to self-actualization, contribution, and the quiet confidence of living a meaningful life. A disciplined lifestyle leads to true freedom, but uncontrolled freedom leads to slavery of the senses.

***

The best gifts of life are not achieved through efforts, but are received with grace. You can build your net-work and net-worth through efforts, but you cannot buy true friendship and love. You can buy the best health plan, but can't buy health. Be grateful for all the gifts in your life, because you did not deserve most of them—you just got lucky!

***

If you have been given a unique talent, it is your divine duty to work on it, to further polish it, and to use it to serve the world. Our service is the rent we have to pay for our stay on this planet.

# The Tree of Inspiration

If you are able to provide strength and comfort to others during times of fear and uncertainty, if you are able to see positive possibilities in the midst of despair and can guide people to take the right actions for a powerful future, if you can see the best in people even when it is not easy and inspire them to achieve their potential, then – my friend – you have the seeds of leadership, and you have the responsibility to lead.

***

As we succeed in life and we start reaping the rewards of our hard work, there is a tendency to get distracted by the rewards. We stop doing the things that made us successful in the first place. We need to maintain our dedication, and work-ethic; keep on learning and growing and keep on taking on new challenges. As suggested by the movie "Rocky, we need to maintain our hunger and "The Eye of the Tiger".

***

Being completely engrossed in a task that you truly enjoy is an amazing feeling. This state of flow has brought to life many important ideas that have shaped the world. This is the moment in which the artist and his craft are one. When you are on this path, the journey and the destination are one. Finding the work that you truly enjoy, are good at, and that can support you financially is the best gift that you can give yourself.

***

Feeling good on a day-to-day basis is critical for our long-term wellbeing. Feeling good has very little to do with our belongings and our achievements. Feeling good is about focusing on progress, accepting some of life's inevitable pains, still appreciating life's gifts, and acknowledging our power to make a difference in the world.

***

Have an open and kind heart, abundant mind-set and positively confident attitude. An open heart ensures free sharing and serving, and helps us to experience the feeling of unfathomable bliss. When we are on our deathbeds, we will take these experiences with us and leave our belongings behind. Focus on the human experience without getting blinded by the quest to acquire more and more things.

***

Success can be seductive, and its charm can sweep you off your feet! We can get so caught up in the trappings of success that we can forget the habits, the discipline, the people and the grace that brought us here. Our fall starts when we lose contact with the ground. Humility, persistence, gratitude and discipline are great companions in a consistently victorious life.

***

A written goal is a contract between the present "you" and the future "you". When the present "you" gets frustrated by the trivialities of life, the future "you" demands the very best through the contract. By having a written goal, and by holding yourself accountable, you create a foundation for a happy and well-lived life.

***

## The Tree of Inspiration

While striving for success, be aware of the sacrifices you are making. Health, once lost, is difficult to repair. It is impossible to repair the bonds with loved ones once lost. The feeling of chronic incompleteness can't be cured by things and trophies. Balance is critical. There is no glory in achievement without someone to share with, and there is no meaning in being a life-long lazy beach bum.

***

Perceived happiness on the attainment of goals is the driver of the world's progress. It is critical that we pursue with passion our responsibilities to contribute to the betterment of the world. However, it is also true that if you are not with what you have today, then it is unlikely you will ever find long-term elation. Hence, we are all tasked with the dual responsibility of fulfilling our roles with passion and gusto while simultaneously choosing to be happy in the present... no matter what!

# Inspiration from Perspiration and Pain

## What we can learn from Fighting the Good Fight, Against the Odds

As we pursue our dreams – whether they be material or spiritual, or ideally both – we face inevitable setbacks along the way. The great Thomas Edison defined genius as 1% inspiration and 99% perspiration. Can we find inspiration in the perspiration we suffer as we fight to achieve our aims? I think so...

---

Eagles soar against the wind and not with the wind. A piece of coal is transformed into diamond through intense pressure. An athlete becomes a champion after grueling practice. An easy life is a life of no significance for anyone. Next time you face a challenge, dig in your heels and face it bravely, persist in the pursuit of your dreams, and never give up. The bigger the challenge, the sweeter the victory!

***

Don't let the challenges thrown by the world weaken your resolve. Within each one of us is a powerhouse hidden deep within layers of fear and doubt. Believe in yourself and never give up. The victory always goes to the one in the arena; the one who rises up after every fall.

***

Keep on moving forward, no matter what comes your way. Be prepared for some heartbreaks, failures and disappointments, but remember that the satisfaction that comes from overcoming challenges is much greater than the pain along the way. Never let go of your dreams, and never stop believing in yourself and your ability to transcend challenges.

# The Tree of Inspiration

A true warrior is not concerned with the glory of victory or the pain of death. He focuses his entire attention on winning the current battle. We are all called to fight our daily battles with our complete awareness and attention. There will be days we win and there will be days we lose. But, no matter what the external outcome, the guaranteed reward is the internal feeling of satisfaction while resting our heads at the end of the day—the feeling that we gave it our all and held nothing back!

***

When you work hard towards a worthy goal and you have a plan that is working for you, you achieve a state of inner joy in spite of temporary pain. This is similar to the last rep of weight training session—it is quite painful, but gives the immense mental satisfaction of working towards tangible health goals. The fun is in the journey.

***

Failures and setbacks are critical steps on the path of progress. Let every failure strengthen your resolve and help you to fix what is not working. Have an unshakeable determination and persistence while pursuing your goals. And never ever give up!

***

Your biggest asset is your self-confidence. Let no one take that away from you. Self-confidence gives us the power to fight against all odds and still move forward. Self-confidence doesn't mean being a braggart. It means the quiet and determined belief that you have what it takes to fulfill your mission in life.

***

## Inspiration from Perspiration and Pain

Doubts, fears, and obstacles are bound to come sooner or later.as you start pursuing your life's purpose. These are tests to test the strength of your desire and willpower. It is very easy to let go of your dreams because of these roadblocks. But when on our deathbeds, will we want to remember a life of comforts but with silenced dreams... or a life in which we gave our all to pursue our life's purpose? Never give up on the journey to the self-actualization that comes from making your unique contribution in the world.

***

There will be times when every fiber of your body will want to give up. You will question the sanity of your dreams. But you have to remember the reason you are fighting for whatever it is that you are fighting for. If you have a strong "Why?", somehow you can withstand any "How?" Be persistent in the pursuit of your dreams, because the world deserves your best.

***

You are more powerful than your circumstances. Don't let any tough situation dampen your resolve. Fight any adversity with every ounce of energy you have. If you never give in, you will emerge victorious. No one can stop you except you.

***

All great achievements come from unflinching determination, willingness to make big sacrifices, and constant victory over self-doubt. We are not here just to live and die. We are here to embrace our unique greatness and make our own mark on the world. Thinking small seems most natural, but it does not help anyone. Let us conquer our fears and step up to create a compelling future so that we can leave a lasting legacy beyond our lives.

# The Tree of Inspiration

You are not given any challenge that you cannot handle. Remember that with every challenge comes the strength to bear it and the creativity to transcend it. We get bogged down because we are unaware of our inner strength. Dig deep and face every challenge head-on, because you are bigger than the challenge.

*** 

We can't have positive growth in our lives unless we are willing to be comfortable with some discomfort and uncertainty. When we voluntarily choose to be uncomfortable for a higher purpose, life becomes incredibly easy because we get the confidence that we are bigger than our circumstances. And no matter what happens, we will prevail.

*** 

There cannot be a victory without some setbacks. Each setback is a test of our belief and persistence! No matter how trying the circumstances, never stop believing... and never ever give up.

*** 

When life throws a tough challenge at us, the first step towards a solution is to strengthen our self-confidence and the belief that we have what it takes to face the challenge. Our best weapon in any battle is our indomitable spirit and our triumphant attitude. If we win the battle within us, no enemy can defeat us from the outside!

***

## Inspiration from Perspiration and Pain

Trials and tribulations are the best teachers. Sometimes life knocks us down, and as we are lying down beaten and broken there seems to be nothing left in us. It is in these moments that we define our life, stand up defiant with every ounce of energy, and resolve to fight back again and again until we win... or die trying!

***

Comfort is the enemy of the achiever. What starts initially as a comfortable option soon becomes very boring. As we try to grow, the initial phase can be uncomfortable or sometimes painful, but as we conquer different milestones on the path, the journey becomes exciting and fulfilling.

***

If there is life left in the body, there is fight left in the will. Let no obstacle crush your will. You are much more powerful than the challenges you face. Look at the challenge straight in the eye and march forward with all your might, crushing all the barriers in your way. You are the victor, not a victim.

***

If you have a worthwhile goal that you are committed to, there is no power in the world that can stop you.

***

When you fall down on the path to your dreams, you might get dejected. You might question your abilities and the plausibility of your dreams ever becoming real. These are the moments to pause, regroup, renew and rejuvenate to get the energy to fight the odds and achieve your dreams. The tougher the fight, the sweeter the victory.

***

There are times in life when we are called to shatter the veneer of comfortable living that wraps and warps our lives. It comes down to the gritty battle of our lives, in which our ideal unlimited selves battle with our incompetent, neurotic and lazy selves. Whoever wins in this battle is going to decide our future of being either a soaring eagle or a timid mouse.

***

The ability to withstand pain while quietly pursuing goals is the most important quality of the champion. In the middle of all the drama, the champion has calm inner silence—practicing what he does best, and transcending pain with a single-minded devotion to his craft. Then comes the touchdown, the home run, and the whole world cheers in standing ovation... oblivious of the painful challenges the champion was silently fighting all along. Be the champion in the arena rather than a spectator in life!

***

The best learning comes from truly tough times. Tough times test the resolve of the strongest. The most natural course is to give up on your dreams and blame yourself for having a higher vision. The universe will not give you what you are due unless it has thoroughly tested what you are made of. Never give up, and fight against all odds to keep your dream alive. Remember that tough times never last, but tough people do.

***

## Inspiration from Perspiration and Pain

You are powerful beyond measure, and much more capable than you imagine. Let no one tell you otherwise. Too often, we sell ourselves short because of self-doubt and the naysayers all around us. Claim your power, take charge of your destiny, and do not stop till you achieve the magnificent goal that your talent is screaming for. You are a victor, not a victim!

***

Focused concentration is required for any worthwhile achievement. When you give it your all for any purpose, no force can stop you from achieving your goal. This also means letting go of everything that is not aligned with your purpose. Don't hold back anything, give yourself completely for your chosen purpose, and then my friend you will surely arrive triumphant on the other side.

***

Don't let fear drown your voice, your dreams and your existence. There are times when you will feel powerless, and that is exactly the intent of fear-mongers. We have to fight back today by doing the best work that we can and by showing extraordinary kindness to unknown strangers. Be unstoppable on your walk to your wonderful dreams.

***

Contrary to the popular opinion, pursuing your passion is not always fun. There are times when you have to use every ounce of energy to continue the race and cross the finish line. The willingness to put in the tough grunt-work differentiates the professionals from the amateurs.

***

# The Tree of Inspiration

The intensity of your determination decides your future. No one promised that life is going to be easy. You will face times when giving up will seem to be the only sane response. But sanity is overrated. Every world-class winner has a streak of insanity within him (or her). The world applauds the crowning glory but is not aware of the sweat and tears behind the scenes. If you are willing to die for your goal, then no one can block your path to victory.

***

Don't lose your faith when times are tough and you don't see the light at the end of the tunnel. Wounds heal and times change. Though you might be scared of the uncertainty, still walk in faith and do the right thing because the situation will turn around and you will emerge triumphant.

***

Amidst all the din and excitement in the arena, the gladiator in the center is in a state of still calmness—totally focused on his goal, and unruffled by the environment. We too are in our own arenas with their own noise and distractions. Don't get carried by the noise, and don't forget your life-purpose. Our maker has given us unique talents and tricky situations to unravel in pursuit of our purpose.

***

Accepting inevitable pain gracefully is critical for one's spiritual progress. If we have a bigger purpose to live for, it is easy to transcend personal pain and to use that pain to strengthen our resolve for fulfilling our life's mission. I heard somewhere that pain in life is inevitable but suffering is optional. I believe that suffering can be reduced by the knowledge that our life purpose is more important than our impermanent life.

## Inspiration from Perspiration and Pain

Every adversity has within it seeds of equivalent or greater benefit. If you encounter challenges, connect to your inner core: the unshakable part of you that has faith and belief that you will overcome. Pray for guidance and think hard to find the seeds of benefit in your situation! Never give up, and put in your very best.

\*\*\*

Nobody promised us that life will be all joy and no pain. Whenever we are in a painful situation, it could be a valuable opportunity to recalibrate our expectations of others and ourselves—to learn new lessons and to appreciate the good moments that are gone and yet to come. These could be the times to fight back, or the times to accept the inevitable. These are the times to pray for acceptance, guidance, and freedom from delusion.

\*\*\*

Anybody who says that the path to success and happiness is easy is lying. There are periods of excitement, times of trial, and moments when you question your sanity. But if you are persistent and focused, you will surely arrive at your destination. Some of the happiness will come from the destination, but majority of satisfaction comes from the fact that you have mastered your moods for a higher purpose.

\*\*\*

It is very difficult to count our blessings when we are in pain. But it is exactly at that moment that we need to count our blessings. Looking at what is working in our lives, and appreciating it, can create the momentum to overcome any hurdle. This momentum creates the energy to either remove the pain or to accept any

# The Tree of Inspiration

inevitable pain gracefully, while appreciating the valuable lessons inherent in the pain.

***

When you are in a painful situation, your confidence can get shaken up and you might not be able to think straight. One way to regain confidence is to alleviate someone else's pain and provide confidence to others. This simple act can give you a better perspective of your pain and increase your confidence to resolve your own situation.

***

In this age of instant gratification, it seems very natural to get out of a painful situation immediately. An exercise which helps me in these situations is to visualize myself as an 85-year-old walking with a stick and looking back at a life of immense contribution. From that long-term perspective it is easier to decide on a course of action. Sometimes the answer is to solve the problem permanently, and sometimes it is better to bear the pain gracefully while fulfilling the long-term vision of a life of contribution.

***

Every painful situation can be interpreted in an empowering way. With a positive attitude, willingness to learn, and an indomitable mindset, breakdowns can be transformed into breakthroughs. If there is a painful situation in your life, think about the lessons you can learn, think about how to prevent this situation in future, and think about the power of prayer... plus the graceful acceptance when you can't change the situation.

***

## Inspiration from Perspiration and Pain

When life is fired by a purpose, physical and mental discomforts cease to matter. Tremendous energy, deep belief and unshakable confidence come to your aid to transcend any obstacles that come in your way. You find yourself in a state of bliss, realizing that many of the obstacles are only in your mind and are not real. If there is one responsibility that we have, it is to go inwards into the depths of our soul to find the pearl of our unique life-purpose.

***

Self-confidence and belief in a powerful future can help to transcend any pain in the present. We might never be able to understand the mysteries of life, but we are all called to live it. If we have to live it, why not live with self-confidence and passion focused on a powerful vision for future? Why not enjoy the ups and downs of this journey?

***

The path to greatness is not easy. There will be times when you have to muster every ounce of energy to move forward. If you have a clear vision of the future you want, and a very strong reason to back it up, you can achieve almost anything that you set your mind to. If you want to grow, but you don't see the results—increase the stakes in the game, burn your bridges, and close all alternative options. You'll have no choice but to plod ahead and win.

***

Within each of us there is a gigantic power to make a phenomenal difference; to persist despite huge challenges, and to walk forward through thunderous storms. Our only responsibility is to believe in this power, and to use it when required!

***

# The Tree of Inspiration

Clarity about long-term goals is critical for withstanding the obstacles and challenges in life. Enormous power comes to the aid of a determined mind. If we find ourselves to be tentative in life, it is because we don't have a goal that inspires us and helps carry us through the battles of life. Look inside yourself and outside at world, press the pause button in your life, and then carefully craft your unique life-purpose. Then spend your life pursuing and practicing it.

***

No matter how tough the situation, learn to wear your self-confidence and always smile. This is the first step to tackling any difficult situation. Strong self-confidence gives strength to others, and a genuine smile-radiated friendship.

# Educational and Inspirational

As already hinted, every setback we suffer can be treated as a life lesson. Our whole lives constitute one big learning experience at what some people have called the "University of Life" or the "School of Hard Knocks". Here's what we can learn in life, and from life...

---

Working alone and trying to do everything by oneself is an ineffective and suicidal strategy. Connecting and collaborating with others to share ideas is the only way to succeed in the new ever-changing world. Create your own "dream team" for success by finding activity partners, individuals with complementary strengths, and mentors.

\*\*\*

An inspired heart is a very powerful force and is behind every major human achievement. Quite often, as we grow older, we lose our inspiration because of the daily trifles of practical living. It is our supreme duty to find constant sources of inspiration – books, people and ideas – throughout our lives. This is required to make our unique life-contributions to the world.

\*\*\*

An interesting aspect of a magical moment is that often we don't realize the magic when we are in the middle of the moment.

\*\*\*

# The Tree of Inspiration

Every pain brings with it priceless lessons. A mean boss, an annoying coworker, a complaining spouse, the rough driver who cuts you on the freeway—they are all teachers telling us that we have not mastered ourselves. If we can learn the lessons and practice kindness when it is difficult, we can tune in to the abundant love and bliss that we came from.

***

Never be afraid of failure. Failure is a much better teacher than success. A successful life is all about constant learning, and by treating every failure as an important lesson we can make our lives worthwhile. Keep on trying new strategies, work on new goals, and welcome new relationships without fear. Life happens on the other side of fear.

***

Great teachers helped us learn in schools and colleges in order to graduate. Life is incredibly more complex, but we are expected to figure out our path through a process of trial and error. Some lessons in life are best learnt on our own, but to accelerate our learning in life, teachers are always available in the forms of books, mentors and guides. If you commit to continuous education through life, life would commit to continuous growth in you!

***

There a lot of lessons we can learn from a dog—loyalty, empathy, unconditional love, and verbalizing feelings. A dog is a friend who never judges you, never gossips about you, never betrays you, and just loves you for who you are.

***

## Educational and Inspirational

Great achievements are not the result of sporadic efforts, but of persistent, small, daily work over long periods... guided by big dreams and great mentors/coaches. There is more than meets the eye with "overnight" successes!

***

It is important to have guides and mentors for every major area of our life: career, health, finances, marriage, and raising children. Often, we don't have natural role models within our family, and hence it helps to seek expertise and knowledge from someone who is really great in a particular area. It takes humility to ask for guidance, but it is better than the pain of a regretful life.

***

Dissect every success and failure to extract the key lessons. Learning these lessons is what gives us confidence. Without the lessons, successes and failures are just temporary highs and lows with no long term significance.

***

Be careful about what you turn your attention to. Even if life throws you a curveball, you can focus your attention on the lesson contained in that experience. No matter how tough the going gets, visualizing a powerful future can give you the energy to move forward against all odds. Think positive thoughts and the journey becomes purposeful and enjoyable.

***

We can learn from nature on how to be actively calm and calmly active.

# The Tree of Inspiration

The critical art of balance is an important lesson to learn. There is a time to strive and there is a time to let go. There is a time to fight and there is a time to surrender. There is a time to mingle and there is a time to be alone. Your intuition always knows the right time for the right action. Listen to its silent voice amidst the worldly noise and then you can know the true meaning of balance.

# Being Grateful is Inspirational

## What we can learn by developing an Attitude of Gratitude

We've dreamed the dream, we've fought the good fight, we've savored every moment, and we've learned some lessons along the way. But besides pursuing our dream goals, sometimes it's good to be grateful for what we've already got...

---

An uncontrolled desire is like a ravenous animal: it never gets satisfied, no matter how much is given to it. If you are clamoring for more without appreciating what you have, there is a danger of dying dissatisfied. That would be a real tragedy because life is a joyful journey and every living moment is priceless... available to be savored as it is.

*** 

If life is a flower, gratitude is its fragrance! Quite often, I hear that I will feel grateful once I get something to be grateful about. My experience has shown me that this actually works in reverse. When we are grateful for what we have, we get more to be grateful about. What are you grateful for today? Find something today to be grateful for, and celebrate its existence in your life.

***

Unless you can appreciate the aspects of your life that you cannot control, you cannot appreciate your ability to control some aspects of your life.

***

# The Tree of Inspiration

The attitude of gratitude ensures an ever-improving powerful future. When we are grateful for little favors, the universe rewards us with bigger favors. If we are alive, have some food and a roof over our heads, we have all the reasons we need to be very grateful. If we have some friends, that is an added bonus—the icing on the cake. When we focus on what is right in any situation, we get the energy to work on what can be improved.

***

I've gone on exotic vacations, to world class concerts, jumped from planes, and checked off items from my bucket list, but I have found that every fulfilled desire creates ten more desires to be pursued. Do I want my life to be a list that I keep checking off, or do I tune into the magic of the present moment? I choose the latter—being in awe of the creation, finding completeness in imperfections, and performing my duties without striving for specific returns. I understand that there will always be wars, killings, lies, vices and malice, but they will coexist with peace, love and honesty.

***

If you can't be happy by yourself, it is highly unlikely that you will be happy with someone else. If you can't be happy with what you have, it is highly unlikely that you will be happy with more. If you can't be happy today, it is highly unlikely that you will be happy tomorrow. Happiness is about finding comfort within yourself, with what you have in the present moment and then do what you can to improve your world!

***

Quite often, when we go through tough times, we wish to go back to the "good old days" when everything was perfect. The fact is that the "good old days" are

# Being Grateful is Inspirational

long gone, and their perfection is a trick our mind plays on us. The only option we have is to forge forward through the tough times and embrace the powerful future that we can bring to life through our courage, persistence and imagination.

***

I have been a non-conformist all my life, and used to get into trouble because of that. Today as I recall some of those times, I am feeling very grateful and relieved that I am a citizen of the USA where there is freedom of speech and expression, where there is respect for people's desire to live their own life, and where there is a framework to foster creativity and reward hard work. I am also very grateful that I don't have to conform to disagreeable norms just to get a paycheck. God bless America and what it stands for! Gratitude for the veterans who fought for liberty and justice for all.

***

You don't have to win an Oscar to be grateful. If you can wake up, breathe, have some parts of our body working, and have food and shelter, this is enough to be grateful. Gratitude doesn't mean that you stop striving to get better; it means that even if the journey of life is tough, you can still be thankful that you are on a journey with endless possibilities!

***

Celebrate the little wins. The little wins are critical for creating a positive momentum. Be grateful for every opportunity, every gift and every relationship. The positive things are here to give us happiness. The negative ones are here to teach us a lesson.

## The Tree of Inspiration

Bragging and gloating about your achievements is counter-productive. Appreciation and gratitude for success and wonderful experiences helps to increase awareness and enhances happiness. But gloating alienates the very people whose support you need to attain higher levels of achievement.

# Inspiring by Loving

## What we can learn from Giving and Receiving the Gift of Love

Where is this all leading? You may wonder. And I can tell you that it's leading... to love. Not merely love for your family, yourself, your friends, or your God, but all of those things. Love is the most powerful force in the universe, and giving the gift of love is the best gift that you can give. So let me inspire you to give the gift of love...

---

When you truly love someone, you can never lose. Even if your love is not reciprocated, your unconditional love can continue to inspire you for a lifetime. Falling in and out of love happens because of the clash between reality and dreamy expectations.

***

It is easier to be a successful human being than to be a better human being. Inner achievements are much more subtle and difficult than outer achievements. But true bliss can only be found when we realize our capacity to love and be loved completely and unconditionally irrespective of our outer achievements!

***

Love is the origin of all life, and yet loving unconditionally is the most difficult thing to do. We might all look and think different, but we are a part of the same universal consciousness. When we hate someone for having wronged us, we create our own prison. You can at least forgive someone and let go, without having to deal with them in future. It will free you up. So let us try to share our love with at least one person today—anyone who is difficult for you to love!

# The Tree of Inspiration

The best gift you can give someone is the feeling that you care for them and understand them. All the knowledge that you can share has no value to the person who believes that you don't care about him (or her). It is much more important to give yourself and your attention unconditionally to the important people in your life than to strive for the adoration of the masses.

***

Anger and resentment are heavy burdens to carry. We might feel strongly about the righteousness of our position and the pain of being wronged, but holding on to that position also locks us out of happiness. Letting go of past hurts, and forgiving others, allows us to embrace the happiness of the present moment. We all have the capacity to love unconditionally, but the expectations of others severely limits our potential to experience abundant unconditional love. Let go, and let love enter our hearts.

***

You are not your achievements, your qualities and your possessions. You are an unconditionally loving soul trapped in the drama of life. Awareness of this perspective while participating in the drama can give you a feeling of deep calmness and serenity... even when you are in middle of tough life-challenges.

***

It is very easy to judge someone who is very different from you, and very difficult to love everyone unconditionally. Loving yourself and others unconditionally is the biggest gift you can give yourself, because only when you love unconditionally can you see the true harmony in nature, beneath the apparent strife and chaos. No matter who you are, how you look, or how rich or poor you are, you deserve unconditional love. Start by loving yourself and then expand to include everyone else.

***

The world is a canvas filled with a variety of emotional colors. It is easy to get sucked into this drama because of our attachments to our egos. But to truly enjoy the beauty of life and creation, we need to let go of our egos and focus on unconditional love for each and every one. When we can forgive others and ourselves, and accept the perfection of the creation within the imperfection of humanity, only then we can connect to the joys of the present moment.

***

No matter what your destination is, take a moment to celebrate your fellow travelers on this journey. These could be people who love you unconditionally. These could be people who drive you nuts but teach you to be patient. If we keep walking in the direction of our dreams, despite the obstacles, we will be farther from where we started. That is success. In the end, life is just a journey, so make it worthwhile.

***

We are all born alone and will die alone. We cannot control the time we have on this planet. But we can control how we choose to live here, irrespective of our circumstances. Our love for others can continue to spread its fragrance even after we are gone. Hence, make every moment count: love others with everything you've got, lend a helping hand to someone in need, offer compassion to someone who needs a little hope, and forgive yourself and others for the mistakes made in the process.

# The Tree of Inspiration

Forgiving ourselves and others for the wrongs done to us is very difficult, but is very critical in order to unravel our true potential. I continue to struggle with it even today. We think we cannot love anyone who disrespects us, but in the long run... we are all dead! Do we want to take a lifetime of anger and resentment to our deathbed? Absolutely not, so let us free ourselves from the shackles of our own creation and open our hearts to a bright and loving future.

***

The desire to please someone whom you love has been the biggest motivating force across civilizations and across ages. If this force can be channeled to worthy objectives for the benefit of mankind, miracles can be achieved.

***

Love has the power to move mountains. I have seen a twinkle in the eye of 95 year old thinking about the love of their life. Anyone who has ever truly loved someone can never lose, because he or she has memories to last a lifetime.

***

Can we solve world's problems? No. Can we make the world a more loving and kinder place? No. Can we ensure that our political parties work in the long term interest of our nation? No. But, we could try to be kinder, more loving and more helpful to the people around us. We can do our best without expecting gratitude. No one might care, but we can live and die with the feeling that we tried to be a part of the solution... not the problem.

# Inspiration All Year Round

### What we can learn from Different Days of the Year

To round off, I'd like to talk about how we can be inspired all year round, and in particular at particular times of the year...

---

May the New Year bring you an abundance of health, wealth and happiness. May the divine grace fulfill all your wishes, dreams and aspirations.

***

Every remarkable achievement results from a combination of divine gift and human will. The simultaneous presence of gratitude for the gift, and the unflinching desire to make things better, results in history being made in every moment. What would you do to make this year the best year of your life?

***

This Valentine's Day, celebrate the unconditional love we have received in life: the love of our parents when we were toddlers, when we had not learnt the science of give and take; the love of our friends who were there for us during our tough times; the spark in the eyes of that special someone. Love adds a special meaning to life, so let us acknowledge it by performing at least one specially loving act for someone today!

***

# The Tree of Inspiration

Love is not just about feeling the tender flutter in your heart when you see someone special. It is also about sacrifice, belief, letting go of the trifles, mutual respect, and holding on when the going gets tough. It is the desire to create a loving and compelling future, come hell or high waters! Happy Valentine's Day!

***

Let us honor those innocent victims and the brave firefighters who sacrificed their lives on this day, September 11th 2001. Terror can take lives but it cannot touch the will and determination of the American people. It is this spirit of liberty, honor, and responsibility that makes America great.

***

Happy thanksgiving to all of you! Thanks to God for life, friends, family, food, shelter, faith, gratitude and for unconditional love despite our errant ways! Thanks for all His gifts that enrich our lives! True abundance comes from sharing. When you open your heart to feel others' pain and help to alleviate that pain, that compassionate moment is the key to your happiness. This holiday season, be a balm for someone's pain, be a Santa for a sad heart, and be the joy in others' life.

***

The best gift you can give someone is to just listen deeply, feeling what they are feeling, and being completely present. Our busy lives and transactional focus are impediments to deep connection. This Christmas, in addition to buying presents, give your loved ones the gift of your presence and listen with all your heart to messages from their hearts. Merry Christmas!

***

## Inspiration All Year Round

We all have worked very hard this year! Now is the time to chill and relax, spending time with family and friends, creating memories, being disconnected from work emails, phones and meetings; giving body, mind and soul time to relax and rejuvenate. Trust me, there will always be work to do and goals to achieve. But time to rejuvenate has to be created too. Happy Holidays to you and your loved ones.

www.ingramcontent.com/pod-product-compliance
Lightning Source LLC
LaVergne TN
LVHW021411080426
835508LV00020B/2552